Relationship Affirmation Cards

ISBN# 9780981891576

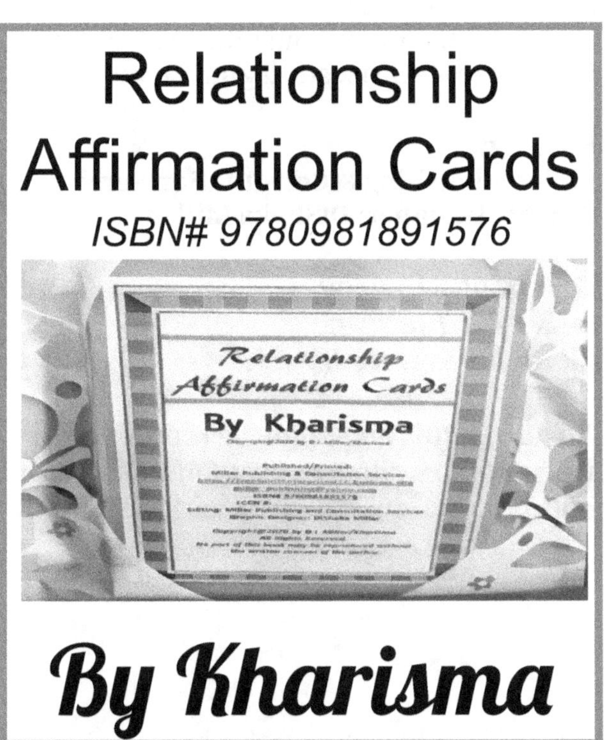

By Kharisma

Published/Printed:
Miller Publishing & Consultation Services
freespiritenterprisesllc@gmail.com

Editing:
Miller Publishing & Consultation Services
Graphic Designer: DiSheka Miller

<u>Acknowledgments</u>

Special thanks go out to the Love Revolution of RVA, my family, friends, long-time supporters and fans.

To Michelle, Steven, Jackie, Marcus,and many others who continue to believe in the power of the *Love Revolution* since 2010.

"The Love Revolution keeps turning..."

<u>Introduction</u>

The purpose of the relationship affirmation cards presented by the Love Revolution is to help enhance healthy relationships and preserve them through tough times.

**Instructions: How to best use these cards
to develop and enhance your relationship**

❖ Shuffle the cards out of order like a
deck of playing cards.

❖ Sit with your significant other with no
distractions. You can use soft music,
candles, incense, etc., to set the
mood, but nothing that is too
distracting. Dedicate to being together
at least 30 minutes uninterrupted.

❖ Take turns reading the cards. Listen
attentively, and respond respectfully
and lovingly.

❖ Use the deck anytime, especially when
the relationship needs reviving or
help.

Challenge!

Tell your partner three or more things that you really appreciate about them. Listen to each other brag about your love for each other.

Think back to the most
difficult point in your
relationship.

Were you able to
move past it, or is it
still lingering?
Talk with your partner
about addressing it if
necessary.

Share a special
moment/event with your
partner like a beautiful
sunset or sunrise.

Plan ahead or go with
the flow.

Meet in your partner's comfortable space, and enjoy being in his/her turf, (with his/her permission of course.)

What is it about your significant other that INSPIRES you most?

Tell your partner
what you love
most about
him/her.

Allow him/her to
reciprocate.

Look at your
mate and find a
new thing you
never noticed
before to marvel
about him/her.

How has your life been ENHANCED since your relationship began with your partner?

**Sit with your
partner with no
particular intent or
purpose. Just enjoy
his/her energy, and
VIBE together.**

Challenge!

Choose three
different unique
activities to do
with your partner.
Encourage him/her
to do the same.

Do you know your
partner's dreams?

What part do you
play in them, and
what part does
he/she play in
yours?

The next time your partner is telling you a story, work hard to "actively listen" to what he/she is saying by repeating back the main points made during the story.

When is the best time to give your significant other space versus giving attention?

How do you best deal with conflict within your relationship?

LOVE

Is Real

Action not

just a **word**!

Who has
influenced your
relationship in a
positive way?

Name them.

Say "My partner is special, because…"

____

____

____

____

____

My significant other's love language(s) is(are)

____

____

____

____

TOUCH
GIFTS
WORDS OF AFFIRMATION
QUALITY TIME
SERVICE

My love language(s) is/are…__________

____

_________________,

and my significant other is aware of it/them.

TOUCH
GIFTS
WORDS OF AFFIRMATION
QUALITY TIME
SERVICE

What draws you in magnetically to your partner?

Eliminate outside
influences in your
relationship.

Who is invading
your relationship
space?

Let's talk about sex!

Describe the last sexual experience you enjoyed with your partner. Repeat it!

Turn to your lover
and show him/her
what you love
most about
him/her.

This can be sexual
in nature or not.

Name at least
three things you
have in common
with your
significant other.

Get that spark
back!

What will make
your
relationship
more exciting?

**Remember, pick
your battles!**

**It is better to be
happy together
than right all the
time. Let him/her
have it sometimes.**

Time to reminisce!

Remind each other of your first time meeting, first date, and first anniversary.

**What differences
do you and your
partner have that
make your
relationship
together special?**

Affection Time!

Grab your partner and hug, kiss, massage, etc. for ten minutes straight.

What's your
magic Formula?

What are the
ingredients in
your
relationship
"cake?"

Compliment Time!

**Take a good look
at your loved
one and
compliment
him/her.**

Keep the spark alive!

Do something sexy and out of the ordinary for your mate.

What does your
relationship bring
to your life?

How does it
enhance your
life?

What is the "glue" that keeps your partner and you together?

Compromise is an important part of every good relationship. How do you and your significant other compromise for each other?

What is your
partner's concept
of mutual respect?

Are you
recognizing and
receiving this in
your relationship?

What <u>affirms</u> your relationship?

What is really good about it?

What is the
most fun you
have had in the
bedroom?

What were you
doing?

Time to Reflect:

Go back to the day you first met. What was that experience like for you? For your partner?

Think for a
moment...
what is a
strength of
your mate that
you currently
lack, and
vice-versa.

What's your
favorite
physical
attribute on
your mate's
body?

Describe your partner's positive personality traits.

What was the
last pleasant
surprise given
by your
partner?

Tell your
significant other
the last thing that
they <u>said</u> that
made you feel
proud of yourself.

Tell your
significant other
the last thing
he/she <u>did</u> to
make you feel
proud of him/her.
Explain.

Remind your mate of your favorite love experience.

What is the "glue" that helps keep your relationship together?

A strong bond
holds relationships
together through
storms and fire.
What bonds you
the most?

Ask your significant other for his/her favorite time with you since the beginning.

Create your own <u>relationship affirmation.</u>

____

____

____

____

____

Set a specific time to
"date' within the
relationship. Also, set
a time to be apart for
yourself.

This will help foster a
greater appreciation
for each other.

THINK

Have these
affirmations
helped enhance
your
relationship?
Why or why not?

REFERENCES

Images:

https://www.pinterest.com/sashalhumphrey/black-love-art/

https://www.self.com/story/quarantine-date-ideas

https://www.whats-your-sign.com/heart-symbol-meaning.html

https://www.shutterstock.com/image-photo/young-couple-having-picnic-park-on-571075438

About the Author...

Kharisma has been self-publishing her novels, books, articles, and essays since 2006. Native to the Metro Richmond, VA area, Kharisma grew up writing poetry, plays, short stories, and school news articles. Later she began to write for online magazines and social media blogs based on various topics from relationships and dating to food and entertainment. After being encouraged by friends and family, Kharisma decided to formally publish her work for others to enjoy, as well as inspire other authors/writers to self-publish as well. Kharisma currently has seven (7) previously published novels and books. This relationship card set will be her 8th title with more titles to come in the near future.

www.ingramcontent.com/pod-product-compliance
Lightning Source LLC
Chambersburg PA
CBHW050000070726
47592CB00019B/1699